cherry docs

DAVID GOW

Cherry Docs
first published 1998 by
Scirocco Drama
An imprint of J. Gordon Shillingford Publishing Inc.
© 1997 David Gow
Revised edition August 2002

Scirocco Drama Editor: Dave Carley
Cover design by Terry Gallagher/Doowah Design Inc.
Cover photo by Paul Martens. Used with permission of Manitoba Theatre Centre.
Author photo by Tim Leyes
Printed and bound in Canada

We acknowledge the financial support of The Canada Council for the Arts and
the Manitoba Arts Council for our publishing program.

Canadian Cataloguing in Publication Data

Gow, David, 1964–
        Cherry Docs
    A play.
    ISBN 1-896239-37-4
        I. Title.
PS8563.O877C44 1998   C812'.54   C98-900886-X
PR9199.3.G6576C44 1998

J. Gordon Shillingford Publishing
P.O. Box 86, 905 Corydon Avenue, Winnipeg, MB Canada R3M 3S3

For L. Kalo Gow

David Gow

David Gow is the author of four stage plays: *Bea's Niece* (PCP), *Cherry Docs*, *The Friedman Family Fortune* (PCP) and *The Flight of Peter Pumpkin-eater* (PUC). His plays have been produced across Canada and the United States, as well as in Israel. *Cherry Docs* has seen translation into Hebrew, Spanish and Polish.

David's writing has won numerous awards and endowments in Canada, most notably the Senior Artist Award from The Canada Council for the Arts. He has also had the privilege of being nominated for two major awards for dramatic literature: the Chalmers Award and Dora Mavor Moore Award. He holds a MFA in Playwriting from York University, Toronto.

David is a member of the Alliance of Canadian Television and Radio Artists, The Writers Guild of Canada, Playwrights Union of Canada, Canadian Actors' Equity and the Dramatists Guild of America.

Acknowledgements

I would like to express heartfelt thanks to the following individuals and organizations for their generous support: Damir Andrei, David Baile, Bob Baker, Louise Botham, Martin Bragg, Jay Broadbar, Glenn Cairns, Dave Carley, Angela DaRocha, Donna Dawson, Katrina Dunn, Rosemary Dunsmore, Bernie Farber, David Ferry, Ian Ferguson, Robert Fothergill, Ken Gass, Ed Gass-Donelly, Stephanie de Gouveia, The Gow-Cooper Family, Kalo Gow, Joseph Green, Michael Healey, Erica Heyland, James Harkness, Brad Harley, Josh & Anne Heilman, Rochelle Hum, Katherine Kaszas, Rachel Katz, Ron Lea, Laurie Lam, Paul Lampert, Hamish MacEwan, Ross Manson, Hrothgar Mathews & Family, Jackie Maxwell, Gord McCall, Kristen McCollum, Steven Moore, Heather Morton, Charles Northcote, Vivian Palin, Jacob Potashnik, Paula Potashnik, Louise Pickett, Thom Richardson, Rebecca Picherack, Teresa Przybylski, Jonathan Rooke, Kevin Rees, Richard Rose, David Rotenberg, James Roy, Judith Rudakoff, Dr. Raymond Rupert, Jason Sherman, Gordon Shillingford, Carole Sheppard, Steven Schipper, Ron Singer, Phil Silver, Sally Szuster, Patty Talbot, Graeme S. Thomson, R.H. Thomson, Iris Turcott, Jill Ward, Ron White, CBC Radio, The Canada Council for the Arts, Canadian Jewish Congress, Canadian Stage Company, Dora Mavor Moore Foundation, Factory Theatre, the Jewish Community Centre (Spadina), Laidlaw Foundation, Metro Toronto Council, Ontario Arts Council, Playwrights Union of Canada, Randolph School of the Arts, Tarragon Theatre, Manitoba Theatre Centre, Toronto Arts Council, Touchstone Theatre, 25th Street Theatre Centre, York University's Faculty of Fine Arts and Dept. of Theatre.

Production Credits

Cherry Docs was first produced by Volcano and Factory Theatre and premiered at the Factory Theatre, Toronto, on April 1, 1998 with the following cast:

MIKE .... Ross Manson
DANNY .... R.H. Thomson

Directed by Richard Rose
Set design: Teresa Przybylski
Lighting design: Graeme S. Thomson
Sound design: Angela DaRocha
Assistant Director: Heather Morton
Stage Manager: Erica Heyland
Production Manager: Rebecca Picherack
Produced by Ken Gass, David Baile, Ross Manson
and Heather Morton
Assisted by Rochelle Hum

Cherry Docs was developed and workshopped by Volcano/Factory Theatre, and in the MFA/Theatre and Playwriting Programme at York University. Ian Ferguson directed and served as dramaturge with Paul Lampert as Danny and Kevin Rees as Mike. The play was Mr. Gow's thesis. Mr. Gow was advised by Robert Fothergill.

Cherry Docs received its American premiere at The Wilma Theater, Philadelphia, on May 3, 2000 with the following cast:

MIKE .... Jason Field
DANNY .... David Strathairn

Directed by Jiri Zizka
Set design: Jerry Rojo
Lighting design: Jerold R. Forsyth
Costume design: Sarah Iams
Sound design: Adam Wernick
Stage Manager: Patreshettarlini Adams
Production Manager: Neil A. Kutner
Casting: Jerry Beaver & Associates and Don Montrey
Dramaturges: Carrie Ryan and Deborah Block

Characters

DANNY Dunkelman .... Legal Aid lawyer, late thirties, Jewish.
MIKE Downey .... His client, twenties, a Skinhead

Production Information

The play takes place in a simple room with a large, heavy glass picture window at the back, as though to another room. There is a steel table, gray and ancient 1940s Art Moderne, three wooden chairs, an aluminum foil ashtray is on the table, and a black rubber waste bucket beside the table.

The characters speak their monologues in spotlights, unheard by one another. The titles and images which are detailed appear in the window, which doubles as a projection screen.

Notes on puncuation: In this script '..' indicates the character is looking for words or has run out of words; '...' indicates a thought before a line or a thought that continues after the line; '—' indicates a definite and sharp interruption or overlap; '-' between words indicates a compression of spaces between words or at times an extended breath; ';' indicates a progression of thought. Full caps indicate importance, intensity and occasionally shouting. This material needs to be played rhythmically.

Foreword

With the creation of *Cherry Docs*, David Gow not only moves into the forefront of contemporary Canadian playwrights, he also presents us with a seminal work on the subject of racism. The plot certainly gets your attention, and has a visceral impact. A Jewish lawyer defends a neo-Nazi Skinhead who has been accused of a racially motivated murder. In the hands of a lesser writer we might end up with a play that begins and ends with the conflict between two diametrically opposed and mutually exclusive philosophies. A play about cognitive dissonance. High concept. Nothing left for us to do but cheer on the good guy as he battles the personification of evil. Fortunately for us, David Gow isn't interested in providing simplistic black and white solutions or easy answers. Like all great writers, he is more concerned with the shades of grey inherent in the complexities of the human condition. His powerful, beautiful, and elegiac writing takes us past our own assumptions and prejudices into an examination of the very heart of intolerance. He is writing about tribes. He is writing about history. He is writing about love. The potential violence that threatens to erupt between Daniel and Michael in every scene is informed not just by the aftermath of one savage act, but by the memory of a thousand years of hatred. And this conflict, at the same time, is heightened by the slender thread that holds out the promise of true forgiveness. Both characters pay a high price for the consequences of their actions, but at the end of the play we are left in the uncomfortable position of wondering if the cost of saving Michael was worth the price that Daniel paid.

There is a belief, or at least a tradition, in Canada that new plays must be developed over an extended period of time, and that everyone involved must "save" the play for the playwright. With *Cherry Docs*, David Gow has not only proved that, yes, sometimes you get it right the first time, he has also presented a challenge for everybody who ends up working on future productions of this play. They will have to rise to the quality of the script. My first encounter with this vivid, epic, powerful writing literally left me gasping for breath.

Ian Ferguson

Title on screen:

The First Day
Winter Solstice

Visual image: A nearly bare tree.

Scene One

Evening, prior to meeting MIKE, winter, DANNY's front porch. Holding a cigar.

DANNY: My wife and I both come from mixed backgrounds. We are both of us made up of a bit of this and a bit of that. I'm a genuine Canuck. I'm an English, Irish, Scots, Belgian Jew. The question I always get is, "How Jewish does that make you?" Or if I say I'm Jewish, then I get, "How Jewish does that make you?" ..I wear a small, gold Mogen David under my shirt, on a thin chain, right next to my skin. I have a keepa in my top drawer, Mezuzah by the door, I work out at the Jewish Y. Privately speaking, very privately, I collect whatever I can find on the Zohar. If anyone pushes beyond that, in what is meant as "polite conversation"; I tell them that I drive a soft top, not a convertible. That usually stops that stream of conversation. My wife is Czechoslovakian or what was Czechos...and Chilean. So we opted when looking for a house to find a locale where there's a real mix to be blunt. We live on a street in the West End where there's every race represented. The United Nations of front porches and gardens. Smoking a small Cuban on the front porch of an autumn's evening, a man comes up the walk to ask, "Where do the coloured people live?"

Now if this guy was White driving an Eldorado
with Texas plates asking where "the coloured folk
live?" I'd say "Dunno." This man is Black and very
tall, he has a hint of British in his accent, but not
from the Caribbean so he must be African. "Are
you looking for the Ethiopian people?" I ask.
"Yes," He smiles laughing, glad that I'm understanding. "There are Ethiopians living there," I say
pointing to a particular house. "Oh," He says,
"What about here beside you?" "No." I laugh, this
is an extended family of Portuguese. I'm not sure
why that's funny, but it is. "Anyone else?" He asks.
"Right around here, that's all, except there's a family from Jamaica over here." "Right" He says.
"Thank you the same," and he continues his search
not happy with the house number where the Ethiopians are at. (Pause.) This is my idea of a small piece
of harmony. (Pause.) I look up and down the street.
Chinese, Portuguese, Mr. Cooper, he's what? He's
actually from Newfoundland.

Scene Two

Evening, prior to meeting DANNY, MIKE's solitary cell. MIKE is barefooted.

MIKE: The foot is extremely sensitive. Have you ever seen those charts for foot reflexology? There are people who believe, it's Asians actually, that the foot is a pathway to the rest of the body. The heart and liver and all the rest, are supposed to be able to be reached through the feet. The foot supports the entire body. Balances the body. The person on top riding around. And what do we do? What do we do for those feet? Do we have concern for them? Do we take care of them? No. We allow them to take care of themselves. We wear crummy shoes made in Taiwan. Cheaply made foreign crap labour. And the feet suffer. Feet. *(Pause.)* Feet are like the White Male in today's society. We can put all the pressure on them. They'll take the load. They'll take the load, hey they're feet. Walk with 'em. Walk on 'em. Walk all over them. They're used to it. They like it. I wear Cherry Docs, eighteen hole, steel shank, steel toe, original-air-cushioned, acid, oil, detergent and…waste-resistant-sole. Combat Model. Combat tread. These boots were developed by a leading German orthopaedic specialist. This man was a scientist, concerned with feet. Balance, wear, comfort, weight, sturdiness, cost, and appearance. These were all factors, in the design of the perfect boot. The perfect line of footwear. Put this boot on, and see how it feels. See how it feels to wear a real fucking boot. Laced up properly you have got enough ankle support to strap a knife to the bottom of it and go skating… Walk up to your average piece of shit wall. Gypsum rock on two-by-fours. Think about where the two-by-four might be; Because you don't want to hurt your foot. Now, test the wall with your foot, see if there's any give at all. That's it. That's your spot. Now firmly, with just a little force, put your foot right through the wall. Doesn't that feel good? That's fucking footwear. If I were to wrap my fist with a small towel and hit you; that's assault with a weapon. So if I was walking around with my fists all taped up like I was a boxer ready for a fight, the police might actually pick me up. *(Pause.)* The steel toe in my boot, in my combat boot, that's a weapon. You better be-fuckin'-lieve it is pal. And nobody says a word about it. Can you see it? *(Pause.)* Can you see the steel?

Scene Three

The next morning, DANNY and MIKE meet, interview room, jail.

DANNY: How many legal aid lawyers have you met with?

MIKE: What do you mean? *(Pause.)* None.

DANNY: How many before me?

MIKE: In my life?

DANNY: I am going to indulge in a little colloquial language for a moment here. *(Pause.)* Don't get fucking smart with me. *(MIKE is taken aback by this.)* That's a little personal commentary, do you understand?

MIKE: Uh huh.

DANNY: No?

MIKE: No.

DANNY: No way am I doing this.

MIKE: What did I do?

DANNY: I don't want to hear 'uh huh' from you. The Court is not going to like 'un huh'.

MIKE: What would you like to hear?

DANNY: I'd like to hear you say, "I understand that you were making a little off the record, personal commentary."

MIKE: I understand that you were making a little off the record personal commentary.

DANNY:	Mr. Dunkelman.
MIKE:	Mr. Dunkelman, sir.
DANNY:	Are you being smart?
MIKE:	No sir.
DANNY:	Don't call me sir.
MIKE:	Right.
DANNY:	Do you know what kind of name Dunkelman is?
MIKE:	I know it's not Irish.
DANNY:	Exactly. It's not Irish, not in the least. It is a Jewish name. Which makes me...?
MIKE:	A person with a Jewish name...?
DANNY:	Right.
MIKE:	You're a Jew?
DANNY:	Is that what I said?
MIKE:	So you're not?
DANNY:	What difference does it make to you?
MIKE:	I'd like to know where I stand.
DANNY:	If they sent you a legal aid lawyer who's Jewish, how would you feel about that?
MIKE:	Works fine for me. Works great when you think about it. Are you any good?
DANNY:	No, I failed. I failed everything. My entrance exams, the bars, that's why I'm working as a lawyer. I'm totally incompetent.
MIKE:	I like your sense of humour.
DANNY:	That's great..

MIKE: Oh. *(Pause.)* Well, I don't mind that you're Jewish i
        that's what you're wondering about.

DANNY: Thank you, thank you so much. I'll wire my
        parents. Better, I'll wire Moses. "Moses tell God
        they're lightening up down here." You are a little
        prick aren't you?

MIKE: So, your parents are Jewish?

DANNY: Fuck you, sport.

MIKE: You're very angry.

DANNY: I don't like Skinheads, I don't like neo-Nazis, and
        I'm not fond of tattoos. *(Pause.)* I think the crime
        you're charged with is..ugly. *(Pause.)* So I'm not
        much inclined to like you. You can ask for someone
        else to be assigned, I think...

MIKE: You don't have to like me, I'm not asking anyone to
        like me.

DANNY: *(Pause.)* That's refreshing.

MIKE: For your knowledge (for the record), I did the
        crime. For the record, I was heavily intoxicated.

        *The straightforwardness of this makes a minor im-
        pression on DANNY. A pause.*

DANNY: ...You say you were intoxicated? Did the police
        test your blood?

MIKE: No. But I think it was pretty obvious when they
        picked me up.

DANNY: What did you drink?

MIKE: A fifth of Scotch and three or four pints.

DANNY: So you were quite inebriated?

MIKE: I was pissed out of my skull.

	Anything else?
	A little pot.
ANNY:	Where did the drinking take place?
MIKE:	At a concert.
DANNY:	Which was...?
MIKE:	By a band called HURC.
DANNY:	Is that something to do with Hercules?
MIKE:	No.
DANNY:	What kind of name is HURC?
MIKE:	It stands for Holy Useful Racial Cleansing. *(Short pause.)* It's a pun.
DANNY:	*(Nodding.)* Yeah, I got that. *(Looks down and writes for a moment. He then looks at a file.)* It says here you were wearing steel-toed, cherry Doc Martens combat boots, is that right?
MIKE:	Yeah, cherry docs. Eighteen holes.
DANNY:	It also alleges you kicked the victim thirty-odd times while wearing those boots, is that right?
MIKE:	Yes sir.
DANNY:	Don't call me sir. *(Pause.)* Why were you wearing those *particular* boots?
MIKE:	Steel toes? It's part of what is a recognizable uniform, Mr. Dunkelman.
DANNY:	Do me a favour. Just don't say my name...okay?
MIKE:	Okay.
DANNY:	*(Handing MIKE a folder.)* Would you mind reading this to me?

MIKE: *(He reads.)* "The victim suffered heavy internal hemorrhaging, and structural damage to the spine, which would have made walking again difficult at best. As well, he had what is referred to as an intellectual impairment, more specifically he was having trouble speaking. The attack is characterized as prolonged, the examining physicians feel it must have lasted two to three minutes." Which is kind of long when you think of it. "He lost sight in one eye as well. He died three weeks after the incident, from related brain trauma."

DANNY: *(A pause, MIKE gives DANNY back the file.)* Anyway Mike, what I'd like to know, to get an idea of how you might present in trial is, how do you feel about this?

MIKE: Can I say something to you?

DANNY: Sure. Are you going to answer my question?

MIKE: Yeah, I will. I just wanted to say you don't look like a Jew.

DANNY: Mnnhmnn. Neither do you. You don't look like a Jew.

(They overlap one another.)

MIKE: I'm not a Jew—

DANNY: You're kidding? Funny, you don't look like a Jew—

MIKE: Knock it off—

DANNY: Are you going to hurt me if I don't—?

MIKE: Knock it off—

DANNY: Okay, Jew boy, anything you say—

MIKE: Would you fucking cut that out—?

DANNY: *(Loudly.)* SO HOW DO YOU FEEL ABOUT WHAT HAPPENED—?

MIKE: *(Overlapping and topping DANNY.)* STUPID FUCKIN' PAKI. We don't need Pakis on this planet anyway..

A long pause.

DANNY: Well that's going to need a little going over. *(Pause.)* I think the gentleman was a South Asian, to begin with. How do you think... What kind of defence am I going to concoct for someone like yourself?

MIKE: What do you mean for someone like..?

DANNY: For someone who seems to feel no remorse, who isn't in the least.. Who seems fairly happy—

MIKE: I feel remorse. I didn't want to kill him. I wasn't trying to kill him. I feel very sorry that he died. *(Pause.)* I think what you're asking is, uh, "How can anyone let alone I, defend a racist, white supremacist, Skinhead, punk" is that right?

DANNY: Let's assume for a moment, that you're dead on the money.

MIKE: I don't want to be defended as any one of those things.

DANNY: Oh?

MIKE: Because those are my ideas if you follow me. They are completely separate from who I am as a person. An individual on trial for an act, an assault. I don't want the movement marked with my crime.

DANNY: You will be very lucky to be convicted of manslaughter, much more likely second degree murder, I'd look for mitigating—

MIKE: I want to be on trial for what I did, are you following me on that?

DANNY: No.

MIKE:	I don't want to be tried as a Skinhead, because then they are trying the movement and not me.
DANNY:	"The movement"?
MIKE:	Yeah. It's a movement. A youth movement.
DANNY:	Listen Mike, a lot of this bullshit makes me very hot under the collar, do you understand? I'm not sure that makes me the best person to argue your defence. Maybe there are lawyers in your movement who could put forward your case more sympathetically—
MIKE:	I don't think so. All I am asking is that I be tried. Not the ideology of the Skinhead movement.
DANNY:	The Crown attorney will prosecute you however he or she can, I would be in the unenviable position of defending you, if we decide on that.
MIKE:	Well. I think you're all right. I think you're a good guy.
DANNY:	I frankly don't think a whole lot of you. I'm inclined to think you're a shit.
MIKE:	That's okay. You're going to help me.
DANNY:	Am I?
MIKE:	Yes.
DANNY:	What makes you so certain?
MIKE:	The kind of person you are.
DANNY:	Which is?
MIKE:	Liberal, a liberal thinker. Checks and balances and everybody deserves a fair trial blah blah blah blah…
DANNY:	Is that so?

MIKE: Is it wrong? Is it a wrong way to think?

DANNY: Faced with someone like you...

MIKE: What kind of person am I?

DANNY: Obviously intelligent. You're not a big planner, I don't think—

MIKE: I could have planned all of this.

DANNY: Between beers? I don't think you did. I think you got swept along.

MIKE: Okay, that's possible...

DANNY: Have you got a little checklist, an agenda for to-day?

MIKE: Yup.

DANNY: So where are we?

MIKE: You tell me Danny Dunkelman, where are we?

DANNY: Where do we stand in all of this?

MIKE: Yeah.

DANNY: We stand in shit.

MIKE: What can we do to get out of that position?

DANNY: (Somewhere else momentarily.) ..Look in every direction first, slowly and without moving.. (More present.) The most important thing is that you not say anything to anyone, do you understand?

MIKE: Because it could come back at us later?

DANNY: Yes. That means anyone is a walking tape recorder, with the exception of me.

MIKE: Can I trust you?

DANNY: You can trust me to perform my duties as your attorney.

MIKE: If I need to talk to someone, can I call you?

DANNY: If you need anything in the way of legal counsel and it can't wait, you can call my office. I'll take you through the preliminary hearing; after that we'll see.

MIKE: We'll see?

DANNY: Yeah, one step at a time.

MIKE: (*Slight pause.*) Thanks, that's great. (*He offers his hand.*) Why?

DANNY: What?

MIKE: Why are you agreeing to represent me?

DANNY: For the preliminary hearing.. I don't know. I guess it's a big challenge.

MIKE: I'm a big challenge?

DANNY: It ain't your eye colour, sweetheart. You're an intelligent kid. On some level, I find it a little difficult to believe this as a premeditated act. Maybe a jury would feel the same way. I'll be in touch, keep your mouth shut and your head down.

MIKE: All right boss. Okay.

DANNY: (*About to leave.*) Have you got a reason for wanting me, on this?

MIKE: (*Smiling.*) Like I said, you're a *liberal.* A humanist, liberal Jew. So—you have to do your very best. In an ideal world I'd see you eliminated. In this world I need *you* more than anyone.

DANNY: ..Eliminated?

MIKE: Basically.

DANNY: Is that all?

MIKE: What else is there?

> *DANNY is silent. MIKE is getting wound up.*

> *(Turning his back on DANNY.)* ..Global Fucking Himey Village..

> *DANNY starts a strange and deep laugh, like the kind of laughter you hear after a car accident.*

You laughin' at me?

> *DANNY continues to laugh.*

What are you—laughin'? What is..?

> *DANNY continues.*

What's laughing supposed to mean?

> *DANNY bangs his hand on the table three times, still laughing.*

DANNY: *(Through a surfeit of laughter.)* Yer killin' me, yer killin' me. YER FUCKIN' KILLIN' ME.

> *Lights snap out on the scene.*

Title on screen:

The Second Day
The Very Dead of Winter, Mid January

Visual image: A city from above, at night in winter.

Scene One

Evening, DANNY's dining room with documents, after the preliminary hearing.

DANNY: I left the court, I drove home. I arrive at home. My wife is working late. I have some time to myself. I put my briefcase under the hall stand in the front hall, and tell myself, that after today, I will not open it. I tell myself that after the day I've had, I don't need to look at this case. The courtroom, that was something else… *(Pause.)* I'm driving home, thinking to myself, it's all right, it will be fast, a fast trial. I'm driving home thinking if I had a few more cases going right now, I'd be doing a little better money-wise. *(Short pause.)* The world looks grey in winter, in Toronto. We don't get enough light. I tell myself; that's why I'm feeling depressed, not enough light. I think, if we save enough, next year my wife and I will go to Chile for a couple of weeks. Break winter's back. *(Pause.)* I'm at home and my briefcase is under the hall stand and I'm not touching it. I go upstairs and pour myself a bath that will be almost too hot to get into. I put in some concentrated herbal extract, the room fills with eucalyptus scent. The Germans make the best bath oils you can buy. I'm reading some crap from the Royal Bank. Mutual funds. I wait for the whole room to be steamy. The mutual fund pitch is wet, but the ink they use doesn't run, mutual funds are that important. Waterproof ink. I get into the bath and close my eyes. Close my ears to the sounds of the world, close my nose to the water by blocking the back of my throat, something I learned on swim team. I disappear under water. A very quiet, very slow moving world. Green with German bath oil. Clouds of bubbles overhead. Hold my breath and count slowly to seventy; and eighteen more; and eighteen more; and eighteen more... *(He gasps.)* I'm sitting in the bath. I suddenly feel as though the whole bath is boiling. Why did I pour such a hot goddamn bath? I'm down the stairs in four, still boiling. I snap open the briefcase *(We hear the sound.)* and start pulling out the papers. I spread them out on the dining room table, one end to the other. There's gotta be something here. *(Pause.)* Depositions, interviews, indexes of evidence, photographs, individuals' statements.. *(Under his breath.)* Oh my God, my god, my god. *(Pause.)* "Show me an opening as small as the eye of a needle...and I will make way for carts and carriages to follow." There's water around my feet on the floor. My skin is on fucking fire.

Scene Two

Evening, MIKE's cell, after the preliminary hearing.

MIKE: I'm making a new tattoo on my left bicep. Something to mark this trial, something that won't wash off. You need a needle; but you can use almost anything in place of one. A staple, a paper clip which you sharpen enough. It's gotta be steel, and it's gotta be sharp, and it's gotta be clean. A pen, like a Bic pen, any ballpoint… You take out the nib and you dip the sharp end of whatever you're using into the ink; then push it just under your skin, not too deep though. Starting there you have a choice. You can make different textures, different densities, shades… Push the metal in first, then rub in the ink after, that's a different way, makes a different look. You blow into the top end of the ink tube, get a little more colour… *(Short pause.)* Go back at it. Does it hurt? I can't tell after a while, something kicks in, some endorphin. The brain has chemicals in it.. Chemicals you can get high on.. It makes you want to.. You know what it does. Today was the prelim. So today's the day I start this new tattoo. Start fresh, all over. It's a circus in that courtroom. It's something I want to get over. I'm making two little shapes here on my biceps, when I flex my biceps they'll move. They'll dance just a little. A little two step. Can you guess? Can you guess what I'd make on my arm..? Let's see… I got the Celtic cross, which is for White Power, and Celts, and the part of me that's Irish. Downey. I got the bulldog for the part of me that's British, my Ma's side. I've got the all important Maple Leaf; which is me right here, right now, my right to be in Canada. Last, and most important: I got a pride of lions, and that's for White Pride. That's my Legion (Chapter), Skinheadwise. What do I need now? I got a red Bic tube, and a black Bic tube, I mix the red with just a touch of black, it comes out cherry. I'm putting two boots on my left arm, just below the sleeve line. They'll dance for you one day. Two Cherry Docs.

Scene Three

Days later, morning, interview room, jail. The sound of two briefcase latches snapping open as the lights come up.

DANNY: That was fucking disgusting.

MIKE: You didn't like that?

DANNY: You're making me into a hack. A cheap stupid hack. I won't have that…

MIKE: How did I..?

DANNY: Don't play stupid.

MIKE: You don't like the Skins being in there..

DANNY: Twelve pair; twenty four combat boots in my courtroom, with me and my client. *(Playing Crown attorney.)* "Murder in the first degree, and for motivation ladies and gentlemen, turn your heads to the assholes in the peanut gallery."

MIKE: I didn't invite nobody, they came.

DANNY: You didn't invite nobody? That means you invited somebody. You're playing at being stupid.

MIKE: I didn't ask them to be there.

DANNY: You've got a "crew" in the courtroom, I'm supposed stand up there straight-faced; tell the room the crime was not racially motivated.

MIKE: You can tell them whatever—

DANNY: No. I can't. I'm not a hack; we do this better,

	smarter, cleaner or I don't do it at all. Where did you go to school?
MIKE:	Mixed.
DANNY:	Last. What was the last place you were in school?
MIKE:	Jarvis.
DANNY:	Okay, grade what?
MIKE:	Mixed.
DANNY:	MIKE, stop fucking around…
MIKE:	Ten mostly, okay? Grade ten, some subjects into other grades, higher..
DANNY:	So; don't play stupid. I know you're not.
MIKE:	All right.
DANNY:	I can't separate out your views, and those of the Skinheads, when they're sitting there like a crew.
MIKE:	It's open to the public.
DANNY:	You looked at them.
MIKE:	They're my friends.
DANNY:	Do you have any idea what kind of time you're looking at if we don't perform some kind of amazing tap dancing routine?
MIKE:	Yeah, a lot of time.
DANNY:	You could be looking at more time than you have lived so far. Got it?
MIKE:	Longer than I've lived..
DANNY:	Before parole. I can guarantee you after that you won't know *how* to live any more. Think about some numbers. How's the number seven thousand

two hundred and ninety-nine days sound? I wonder what the music will sound like then?

MIKE: C'mon.. I get the picture…

DANNY: I wonder how it would feel to be a forty year-old man, who knows nothing but prison. You'll never get laid again, without a couple of hundred bucks to spare.

MIKE: That's a lot of time.

DANNY: You're not a juvenile anymore, and this isn't a little scrap at the Jarvis High School dance.

MIKE: You saw about that..?

DANNY: Your juvenile record, yes. Quite a career you've built.

MIKE: That guy pushed me.

DANNY: He was Black.

MIKE: Yeah. *(Pause.)* They got gangs.

DANNY: He got stitches. There's always going to be someone pushing you. Jarvis, wherever…

MIKE: …Where did you go to school?

DANNY: University of Toronto, Law… It was near where my..

MIKE: Your what..?

DANNY: Nothing.

MIKE: Something.

DANNY: Near where my parents, at one time in the past, lived. My father.. *(Out of his large briefcase he pulls a very weathered, leather dossier. It could be any age at all.)* I've brought you a dossier. See this? It's a dossier, I had to get special permission for you to have this..

MIKE: What's it for?

DANNY: Your briefcase. Your version of a briefcase. They won't let you have one like mine. The steel, the steel in the hinges, in the snaps, the side guide. Apparently they don't want you to have steel.

MIKE: Weapons? Right?

DANNY: Whatever.

MIKE: People make weapons from anything inside…

DANNY: I don't want to know about it. Concentrate on this. (*He points to the dossier.*)

MIKE: What do I need it for?

DANNY: Every document I have, you have. Every piece of paper, transcripts, statements of..import, everything from your juvenile career. Look through it thoroughly, don't miss a thing.

MIKE: Danny, where are you going with this?

DANNY: This is your case book. You're going to need it…

MIKE: Why?

DANNY: Because you're going to be involved in this, very involved, or I will walk.

MIKE: I'm going to be involved in this trial?

DANNY: Wake up. One way or another, yes.

MIKE: That's your job…

DANNY: I'll worry about my job and how to do it. And, I'll tell you what your job is…

MIKE: Danny, the courtroom, they got me. They got a lot.

The Crown, he's what, Solomon? Jewish. You; Jewish. The magistrate—

DANNY: The magistrate?

MIKE: He looks a little bit—

DANNY: He's Irish. A very old Toronto, Black Irish clan of lawyers. Three generations.

MIKE: Oh...

DANNY: Never can be too sure with a dark barrister, huh?

MIKE: This is your world. This is multiracial Toronto—

DANNY: The word is multicultural—

MIKE: That's newspeak.

DANNY: GUARD.

MIKE: Wait.

DANNY: GUARD.

MIKE: Don't go.

DANNY: Why?

           Pause.

           So you've noticed there's a few Jewish lawyers in the system?

MIKE: Yeah, a few..

DANNY: Tell me something, what were you doing when you were twelve?

MIKE: Twelve? I played street hockey mostly...tennis balls.

DANNY: That must have been sweet.

MIKE: What did you do?

DANNY:	I used that case, after school almost every day after school and weekends. It had all my papers in it.
MIKE:	For what?
DANNY:	I was learning how to read and do a little writing..
MIKE:	At twelve?
DANNY:	Torah study. I was learning how to read one of the world's more ancient languages, how to pray, certain prayers and songs…
MIKE:	Do you think that makes you better than me?
DANNY:	*(Pause.)* You're in jail. *(Pause.)* I'm visiting. You hurt someone deliberately and he died. *You* are in a stinking mess. It's going to take work; study, and energy on your part to get out of it.
MIKE:	Maybe I could try.. I don't know where you're going with this..
DANNY:	You pick the direction. You review the material. You review your record, read everything, and tell me what's the right way to go.
MIKE:	What am I gonna come up with? You're the lawyer.
DANNY:	Right. I'm the Kike lawyer you've gotta play street hockey with now. If we're not a team we both go down.
MIKE:	I want to think about this.. *(Rubs his arm, his tattoo, until a bloody scab appears.)*
DANNY:	What's that on your arm? You get into a scrape?
MIKE:	No, I know how to be incarcerated. *(Pause.)* It's just a thing..a symbol.
DANNY:	What is it?
MIKE:	Nothing yet, it's not finished.

DANNY: Why don't you just tattoo "guilty" across your forehead?

MIKE: ..I was bored.

DANNY: Well now you have some reading material. There's about four hundred pages there, related directly or indirectly to you.

MIKE: ..My point of view, that we're losing Canada; that we're losing the English-Canadian White way of life, that's something I want to hold on to separate from—

DANNY: It's not separate—

MIKE: If multiracial societies worked they wouldn't have to sell it to us with tax dollars, for millions a year—

DANNY: …MIKE.

MIKE: Millions of immigrants a year—

DANNY: Maybe that's your angle. Think about it, maybe you want to get up there and say you resent the hell out of what's happening to this country. Maybe that *made* you do it. I am going to want a precise, logical, cogent argument from you. You okay with those words?

MIKE: I understand what you're saying, but I—

DANNY: I don't want to hear about it. Read through all this material carefully, I'm not meeting with you again till you've done that. Not until you come up with an angle of attack.

MIKE: What if I don't.. if I can't do this.

DANNY: You can do it, you will—

MIKE: What if I don't want to—

DANNY: *(Laughing.)* Mike, even if I walk, someone else

	would be in my seat.. You want me to play hack to your idiot, I'll tell you how that one would go—
MIKE:	You mean if we keep these issues separate—
DANNY:	If we don't come up with something.. Some kind of approach. You're not using your head, you might as well have stewing beef in there.
MIKE:	Stewing beef, where do you get that?
DANNY:	My.. Here's how it goes with me playing hack to your idiot. I make at least seven thousand from handling you, badly. You go to jail for a long time. I take eighteen percent of my seven thousand dollars, put it in an R.R.S.P. This guarantees that when you get out, I'm playing golf somewhere nice in Florida.
MIKE:	I get the picture..
DANNY:	No, no. I want you to hear and know what a Kike lawyer does with his money, you might learn something. I buy a cigar from the Socialist Republic of Cuba, thirty dollars, smoke that one lazy afternoon. I take a couple of hundred off the top and take my wife to a restaurant you can only ever *look* into. A reataurant that wouldn't hire you as a dishwasher. I take my wife home from the restaurant, we laugh, and get along famously and make love, while you're fending off advances from men. I put a couple hundred aside—my kid's college fund. Getting a clearer picture?
MIKE:	Yeah..
DANNY:	We don't want anyone saying there was a conspiracy, that you didn't get a good crack at the bat. Worst case scenario, they declare you a dangerous offender and you never get out, never even have someone to play cards with or tell a dirty joke to..
MIKE:	ALL RIGHT. Jesus, talk, talk, talk, talk, talk.

DANNY: You're gonna have to do a lot of talking..

MIKE: I'll look at the papers..

DANNY: And you'll start formulating a cogent, brilliant de-
            fence strategy..

MIKE: I'll.. Okay.

            A silence.

DANNY: *(Quietly, almost tenderly.)* Let me show you a little
            something about this dossier. This belonged to my
            dad, he brought it here before the Second World
            War; a time you seem to have indicated some pass-
            ing interest in. Look at the stitching: that's nice Old
            World full-process work. An awl through the
            leather, pushed through with a punch from the
            heel of a hand, handstitching, needle and thread,
            neddle and thread.

MIKE: You're giving me this..?

DANNY: I'm lending it to you, for now. We'll see how it
            goes.

MIKE: All right, I'll read the stuff.

DANNY: And you'll come up with a strategy.. I want your
            brain out of neutral. I want you engaging life on
            some level..

MIKE: I'll do my best.

DANNY: You'll have to do better than that, much, much
            better.

            Pause.

MIKE: Hey Danny, what's it like outside?

DANNY: Colder than hell.

Title on screen:

The Third Day
The Last Day of March

Visual image: A tree branch, covered in buds.

Scene One

Day. MIKE's solitary cell. MIKE is making sounds on breath.

MIKE: Hey-hey-hey-hey-hey-ho-ho-ho-ho-ho-oi-oi-oi-oi-oi. Placing the soles of my feet 'gainst one wall, the heals of my hands against the other, nine-by-six, nine-by-six, nine-by-six, nine-by six..the heels of my hands, the soles of my feet-both walls, facing the floor and *shoot* up-the-wall. Exercise? Ya' could sell it. Up and down. Climb. Up to the top, wet toilet paper on the back-my neck. Soggy wet, toilet paper there. Take it up. Plaster some 'gainst the speaker grill, little too noisy-with-all-the-little-such-and-such. Crawl back down. Keep-it-real-clean-in-here-you-get-away-with-more. Flush the toilet, flush it, flush it over and over. Stainless steel toilet and sink, one piece-it's-a-one-piece-bath-one. Flush it eighteen times, water's cold as ice. Blister cold. Take my shorts, my boxers. Put 'em in there. Cool, cool water-back-the-neck-drive-away-a-headache. Medicine, what's medicine? When ya' got none, nothin. Cold shorts-back-of the neck. Done. Climb back up the wall, fresh wet cold shorts, stuff a corner-shorts in the corner ventilation vent. Humidifier. Humidify the air some.

Gotta have games, gotta have somethin'-nuthin else. *(Pause.)* Now the air's wet, 't's the next day. Now with your thumbnail you can peel moist paint off the old door frame, peel it, scratch it off. Make a little picture, make a little initials. Little scratchy animal. Shave. Face, Head. Half an-hour-forty-five-minute-job. Now it's study time. Look at what Danny said, look at the case, my briefcase. Make a call, collect call to Danny. Fuckin' North Pole freeze out action here. Fuckin' North Pole. *(Pause.)* You know what happens when people talk to you like you're stupid all the time. *You* start to think you're stupid. You start acting *really* stupid. You get pretty angry from it. Who knows where it starts? I gotta start over somehow. They never wanted me in with the regular prison population. Too much danger for everyone with me being a "racist" and everything. Nice huh?

Scene Two

End of the day, waiting area, inside security, jail.

DANNY: I was raised with a certain amount of...an assumption about my own tolerance, about what I thought. Driving to the Don Jail today, to see Mike... It's sunny and not too cold; the end of March. How's it go? March in like a lion, out like a lamb. Kids are playing practically in the traffic, running between the cars. Broadview's a mess, you can't drive on it. Everybody is parked with their motors running. A few feet a minute. So I split off onto a side street. I don't want to be late. I'm going south at about three times the rate I would be on Broadview. I come to a spot where there's a car parked on the wrong side of the street. Cars on the right, car on the left. I have to slow to nearly a stop. I get my car between the two cars, with a foot to spare on either side. Only then I notice four teenagers who've been walking along. They're looking at me, I look at them and smile, thinking it's funny someone needs to nearly block the road by parking on the wrong side. They look to be laughing at the car, parked. We're all sharing a laugh. Four young 'African-Canadian' hip-hoppers and I. They're wearing the hip-hop stuff. The really big pants, big shirts, big jackets. They look like nice kids. We're all smiling. One of the kids gestures to me that maybe I could give them a lift down the block. It's a long block. I'm thinking yeah, hey, what would that hurt? So that kid runs around the back of the car very quickly and he pulls at the passenger door handle. He's smiling. The door is locked. All four doors all the time when I drive downtown. As a matter of habit. He pulls at the door handle a couple of times, still smiling. I reach over to open the lock, I'm going to open the lock, I'm going to open the door to this kid, and I'm actually leaning over with my fingers on the lock switch when I catch in my peripheral vision, movement in front of the car. I look up and there's two of the kids, they don't look angry or anything but they're not exactly smiling. My fingers come off the lock switch. I look in the rear view mirror and the fourth kid is standing behind the car. *(Pause.)* I'm not in a good spot. The kid on the passenger door clicks the handle twice more. I look at him, he's still smiling. "C'mon," he says, "Open the door." I just look at him, try to assess. "Just give us a little ride..." I'm thinking about it. I look at the guys in front of the car. "C'mon," they start saying, "Open up." I decide that is not going to happen. I shake my head 'no' at the guy on the passenger door. He makes a sad face. I smile, and shake my head 'no' again. The guys in the front aren't looking any happier. The car is still in gear. I take my foot off the brake, the car starts to move slowly. The guys in front don't move. The guy on the passenger side let's go of the door. I tap my horn, and the guys in the front don't move. I put my foot on the brake, I calm myself, I gesture firmly for them to get out of the way. They're standing five feet off the front of the car. I put my foot on the gas hard, the tires shriek and spin, the car lurches forward, the guys jump back out of the way. My car takes off down the street. In the rear view mirror I see the guys are standing there laughing, they're laughing hard. My heart is racing. Are they having a little fun with me? With the White lawyer, in the old Volvo. What if the door hadn't been locked? *(Pause.)* I'm waiting to see Mike, at the Don Jail, and all I can think about is... What am I *thinking?* Where is my brain? I'm thinking about punching the shit out of him. I'm thinking about hitting him, and maybe knocking some sense into him. That's what I'm thinking.

Scene Three

End of the day, interview room, jail.

MIKE: Hey.

DANNY: What?

MIKE: Are you annoyed with me?

DANNY: I'm annoyed...

MIKE: With me?

DANNY: I... I haven't even seen you yet, how could I—?

MIKE: You didn't take my calls.

DANNY: ...Only this last week.

MIKE: I needed to speak with you.

DANNY: ...And it couldn't wait?

MIKE: It did wait.

DANNY: Have you put anything together, from your brief?

MIKE: First, what are you annoyed about?

DANNY: Something that happened on my way here.

MIKE: Yes?

DANNY: I don't want to talk about it.

MIKE: Okay.

DANNY: What do you need?

MIKE: I needed to talk to you because...well I, it's uh...

DANNY	Yes, for chrissake what is it?
MIKE:	I'm thinking, I've been thinking.
DANNY:	Okay; Good. *(Pause.)* Have you read all the documents I gave you yet?
MIKE:	Yes, I've read them over—almost, practically, every day.
DANNY:	And?
MIKE:	I don't know...
DANNY:	WHAT? You've been saying that now, going on three months.
MIKE:	I don't know where...or how to start with it all.
DANNY:	You have to start somewhere. What have you got?
MIKE:	I...well.
DANNY:	Yes.
MIKE:	I don't... I haven't got anything.
DANNY:	Nothing?
MIKE:	Essentially. That's right
DANNY:	You read everything?
MIKE:	Yeah, all of it.
DANNY:	Everything you need in order to... What did you call me for, then?
MIKE:	I needed to talk to you.
DANNY:	I told you unless.. About what?
MIKE:	To get some ideas of...
DANNY:	I'm not giving you ideas. Your ideas are what we're dealing with here. Your thoughts.

MIKE: I had to see you. To talk with about what you thought.

DANNY: For the moment it's irrelevant, what I think.

MIKE: Okay, but you could suggest...

DANNY: DID YOU JUST CALL..? Did you just call me down here to yank my chain, you little moron.

MIKE: I'm not a...

DANNY: I know, I know... I expected more. I thought you would have... SHIT. You've been sitting here a very long time. Four months. An eternity, for someone your age. NO FRESH..? No fresh fucking thoughts?

             A pause.

MIKE: You're really, really annoyed.

DANNY: YES. It's a hell of a day. It's a day in the city, and it's getting to me that's all. I told you not to call me again without having something new to—

MIKE: You're not making it easy for me.

DANNY: It's not supposed to be easy...

MIKE: *You're* not supposed to make it hard.

DANNY: All right. What are you going to do next?

MIKE: ...When?

DANNY: When do you think? Now. You have thirty days left to come up with a strategy—

MIKE: I...? How can it be just me? How come you aren't doing your job.

DANNY: Mike. I do my job. I do it every day. I do it at the expense of my home and life where necessary. I already got my degree. We don't need to test my abilities or thought processes—

MIKE: Okay, I know…

DANNY: How can you have read the material and not..?

MIKE: What?

DANNY: How can you have read all that material and not come up with even a little tiny idea to start. …A place to start.

MIKE: Some people think I am stupid, you said "moron"…

DANNY: I didn't mean it, I lost it…

MIKE: Maybe I'm too stupid…

DANNY: Would you cut the self-pitying, dying baby seal crap, please?

MIKE: …Yeah. I will.

DANNY: I have a couple of minutes…a little time left. I've gotta meet my wife, for dinner out. What do you want to do with it? It's your time, paid for already, in my agenda book.

          Pause.

MIKE: Well, for starters, I hear nothing from my Skins…

DANNY: Mike… I will not console you for one second more. What is it, your Skins? The boys in Docs, a tribe of ill-educated, white-trash-sons-of-bitches who have as their strictly avowed purpose the annihilation of the memory, of a people who have already been killed once…

MIKE: I didn't mean to get you—

DANNY: *(Interrupting immediately.)* Who want to shit on the graves of my ancestors. Who would prefer to wipe out my race, for nothing more than blood sport, because they're too stupid to make a go of it for themselves in the best possible part of the entire world...

MIKE: What the fuck happened to you today?

DANNY: SHUT UP. Are you getting me? This is the last stop for this little bus. Are you going to get your head in gear and build me a sharp, resilient, mechanistic, fully functioning defence, or not? Do you have trouble understanding me?

MIKE: No. No, the last question. Yes the first, yes I am totally with you.

          A silence.

DANNY: I don't want to be made a fool of in court again.

MIKE: Okay.

          A pause.

DANNY: Do you understand what will happen in there? They take you apart, your head, your emotions, your soul, your history, they stamp around in that stuff. They take kicks at your thinking. They try to divine who you may one day be... You ever hear about what the Romans did with birds?

MIKE: I'm not sure.

DANNY: They pulled them to pieces, looked at their guts to determine the future.

MIKE: That's sickening...

DANNY: The court pulls you to pieces, and you can't break, can't waiver from whatever defence *you* construct. They will not stop simply because you admit guilt. You have *thirty days* left. You have wasted one hundred and twenty so far.

MIKE: Okay..

DANNY: You are going to have to get into your feelings. Past and present. This is not simple for anyone. …You're going to have to…recognize an honest emotion if it jumps up and bites you in the ass.

MIKE: I have feelings still.

DANNY: A good starting place.

MIKE: I like you… I think you're very smart.

DANNY: (Pause.) I think about hitting you.

MIKE: You do?

DANNY: I feel like punching you, knocking sense and beating logic into you.

> MIKE gets up, puts up his fists as guards.

MIKE: Here, why don't you?

DANNY: No, no.

MIKE: Go on, it'll get rid of the feeling.

DANNY: I said no.

MIKE: C'mon Danny let's go.

DANNY: I'm a lawyer, a, uh, barrister, I can't, the guards.

MIKE: You're a bastard, let's go.

DANNY: No.

MIKE: Danny, even a liberal can throw a punch now again. C'mon, up and at it. (Pause.) Did you hear the one about the Jewish Comedian who lost his sense of humour? It got all burnt out in the "Hoaxacaust."

> DANNY attempts a hollow laugh. Gets up slowly

he moves to where MIKE is standing, he stands very close to him, he speaks very softly.

DANNY: Mike, sit down.

MIKE: Why not?

DANNY: I said sit down, now.

MIKE: I want to know why..?

DANNY: If I started hitting you I might not be able to stop.

       A silence.

MIKE: Now you know how it feels. *(Short pause.)* That's my starting place.

Title on screen:

The Fourth Day
Passover

Visual image: Crocuses in bloom, on brown grass.

Scene One

Evening, DANNY in his dining room, the desk doubling as his table again.

DANNY: I'm red lining it on this. I'm at the wall. I'm digging up all the case law that can be found anywhere, on race-related offences. The hours going into it are incredible. My wife, Anna, has taken to calling me "The Caped Crusader" an ironic piece of humour. The name has spread to my firm. It's starting to wear a little thin...the cape that is. Colleagues ask me bluntly why I'm working so hard on such a case. Why so much resource? I get the odd look. I get the odd look at the Jewish Y, friends who know me. I get the odd look from my wife. I've contacted the Canadian Jewish Congress and have arranged to have a witness testify on the indoctrination of kids as Skins. How these kids get dragged down into this mud and shit. *(Pause.)* I'm working at home, from dinner on. That happens quite often, but it is particularly bad on this one. My wife tells me she's getting to be fed up, I tell her next Friday's likely to be the last day in court. My wife lets me know that it's a good thing, she's really quite sick of this case. I tell her again, tomorrow's likely to be the last day; only wrapping-up after next week. Twenty minutes after dinner my wife starts playing dance music from Chile. Very, very loud. I ask her to please turn it down. She accuses me of not liking dance music from Chile. I tell her I am positively nuts about dance music from Chile, when I'm not trying to get all the concentrative power I have back together. She goes back downstairs and turns it up. The windows are humming. We talk again, the music stays just as loud. I go to the mall and work in the food court for an hour; at the end of which I ask myself point-blank: Am I grand-standing? Is my ego a little too involved in this one? Yes, is the answer. Am I risking the respect of some of my colleagues? Yes, is the answer. Is my marriage at risk because of my working on this case? Yes, is the answer. Is my marriage at risk? Yes, is the answer. Where would I be today without my background? How far could I fall, and what would it take, to take me off my balance? Enough questions. I go home. We dance for half an hour. We make love. I feel good today. The week after next it's almost over; for me.

Scene Two

Lights up on MIKE, sitting on the floor. He smokes a cigarette, from start to finish. He smokes very fast. He is silent and begins to smoke a second one, almost as fast. Lights out.

Scene Three

Night, DANNY in his dining room, the desk doubling as his table again. Putting away the last of some work. A glass of red wine half-filled. A black velvet bag.

DANNY: I can't sleep. Tomorrow is Passover. We're missing it completely this year, my Ma in Ottawa. *(Short pause.)* In a small black velvet bag, that usually I keep inside—what was my Dad's leather dossier. Inside the velvet, a keepa and a prayer shawl that was my Dad's-which-he brought-over-with-him, pretending at times it was just an ordinary scarf. *(Pause.)* I open the shawl on the table, unfolding and unfolding. I lay it out flat. The oil of my father's skin, the back of his neck, almost sixty years against the cloth; yellowy-grey. His smell. His smell throughout it: Almonds—is how he smelled. *(Long pause.)* What texture? What weave? What delicate thread is this? I stroke my father's shawl, hands out to the left, and out to the right. *(Pause.)* I... *(Short pause.)* Inhale my father. Black stripes. How do you make such a pattern? *(Pause.)* At the edges, both edges, which I fold over to the middle, moving it in on itself, and in on itself, the vertical threads simply stop. Stop. Here, strand after strand after-strand of horizon...of horizontal thread, loose-tied-together-the-tiniest-of-knots. Tied by father's thirteen-year-old fingers he told me. *(Pause.)* This cloth, filled with my father...you could practically wring him out of it into a tub of cold water.. At the four corners, re-enforced by a material that looks like pieces of a parachute. Though it's not. I asked more than once. Through these four corners, eight thick strands through each. Silken rope. The eight strands—tied into five ornate double knots. Ten knots per corner, from eight strands. Days of knotting, days of tying.. Ten knots: "That ye may remember and do all my commandments, to affect the mending..and to be holy unto your.. *(Pause.)* God."

Lights out.

Scene Four

Daytime, a week before the trial, the interview room, jail. DANNY brings the third chair forward to the table as the lights come up.

MIKE: Who's that for?

DANNY: Uh..

MIKE: You expecting someone?

DANNY: Possibly..

MIKE: Who?

DANNY: It's a Passover tradition, set an extra place, a glass. Let's get started. You have your dossier?

MIKE: Yeah.

DANNY: You've formed some kind of defence..?

MIKE: I think so. I've done what I can. I'm sick of it. I am sick to death. I have confessed to everything. What more do they want from me?

DANNY: We'll see.

MIKE: Do they want me to sign a piece of paper which says I'm no good. That I'm waste in the system?

DANNY: I don't think that's what they're after.

MIKE: I know that's what I am right now, for them. A wasted person. A waste of a body.

DANNY   Lighten up on the self-pity.

MIKE:	It's like a rack I'm on. They keep turning the wheel a little bit more. "Tell us about your tattoos—"
DANNY:	This is a very, very fine needle we're trying to thread here.
MIKE:	I can feel that.
DANNY:	It's only going to work if you stay with me. I'm going to take you through some of the questions you might be asked. By the prosecutor, by myself, and also by the court.
MIKE:	Right.
DANNY:	I'm not going to be nice. Next Friday, I'll be pleasant. The prosecutor will not. He will try to bug you. He will look down on you.
MIKE:	Yeah I got that much. His cracks about my tie, my new suit...prick.
DANNY:	You can expect more of that. Let's go.
MIKE:	Yup.
DANNY:	Good Morning Mr. Downey...
MIKE:	And I say what?
DANNY:	Try "Good morning."
MIKE:	Start over.
DANNY:	Mike.
MIKE:	Good morning.
DANNY:	How long have you been incarcerated on this charge?
MIKE:	Five, going on six months now.
DANNY:	And you have been where?
MIKE:	Administrative segregation, Don Jail.

DANNY: Have you any family or friends in the Court today?

MIKE: I think maybe Jill's gonna come, maybe Mom
            again.

DANNY: Answer.

MIKE: My mother is here. Jill is also, my fiancée Jill
            Healey.

DANNY: She's your girlfriend?

MIKE: We're engaged.

DANNY: Oh?

MIKE: Yes, to be married.

DANNY: At some point in the future?

MIKE: Hopefully yes, when I get out.

DANNY: You're looking forward to a better future?

MIKE: Yes, I'd like to have a good life.

DANNY: Do you think it's right, that you can look forward
            to a future?

MIKE: I think..

DANNY: As compared to your victim, who is dead. His fam-
            ily, not so much future right now..

MIKE: How can I answer, where's the—

DANNY: What do you have to say?

MIKE: I've been through a certain amount. I don't like
            what I've done and I...

DANNY: Don't go on too much.

MIKE: What?

DANNY: Try to keep the answers concise, short.

MIKE: I was explaining.

DANNY: We don't want too much explaining from you, it clouds things.

MIKE: Okay.

DANNY: What have you been through?

MIKE: The crime I committed.

DANNY: Which was?

MIKE: The assault, which is being charged as murder in the first degree.

DANNY: What have you been through?

MIKE: ...I'm not sure what to say. Realizing what I've done is wrong.

DANNY: Jesus, that's not going to do anything.

MIKE: What's wrong with that.

DANNY: The answer is too short, you're not saying anything.

MIKE: What happened to concise?

DANNY: Just answer the question.

MIKE: What was it again?

DANNY: What have you been through?

MIKE: (Pause.) I've been thinking and I realize how wrong I was. How much I went off any kind of normal path. My action was criminal, and it was influenced by what—

DANNY: I've told you before, don't make excuses. Talk about what you feel, what you want for the future, what you are going to do...

MIKE: Danny... Concise, more, this, that, which is it?

DANNY: All of them.

MIKE: You're trying to piss me off right?

DANNY: Yes.

MIKE: You see um.. it's not ah.. working?

DANNY: Try not to say 'um', or 'ah'. Mouth sounds in general make you sound stupid.

MIKE: Make *me* sound stupid.

DANNY: Yes *you* in particular. You sound stupid, making stupid mouth sounds.

MIKE: I'm not stupid.

DANNY: Don't argue.

MIKE: ..You're not going to get me.

DANNY: What?

MIKE: You're not going to get me to respond.

DANNY: I want to make sure, it's a fine needle we're threading. Answer the question.

MIKE: It, I...

DANNY: What are you STUPID? Think.

MIKE: It's not going to be as bad as this.

DANNY: It's going to be worse. Answer the question.

MIKE: Stop pushing me.

DANNY: No. I'm going to push you much further—

MIKE: All right.

DANNY: Do you consider yourself to be white trash?

MIKE: They can't ask that?

DANNY: Are you white trash?

MIKE: I come from a working class, white upbringing.

DANNY: Is that white trash?

MIKE: No. It is not.

DANNY: What is white trash?

MIKE: It's what's called a derogatory term.

DANNY: Who does it describe?

MIKE: White people, with no school, who act badly.

DANNY: Are you white trash?

MIKE: I don't like to think of myself that way.

DANNY: Are you though? You fit the description.

MIKE tenses at this.

We're waiting.

MIKE: I said, no, I am not.

DANNY: What are you going to do with your time in prison?

MIKE: Get whatever education I can take from the system.

DANNY: WHAT?

MIKE: Take advantage of the opportunities for education, to finish high school to begin with, and whatever else I can.

DANNY: Okay.

MIKE: I will take what I can, like all good white trash.

A silence.

DANNY: Longest possible sentence, twenty-five years to parole.

MIKE: Oh.

DANNY: One joke, I'll kick the shit out of you, I swear.

MIKE: Who's getting angry?

DANNY: I'm allowed. I'm not being assessed.

MIKE: Keep asking...

DANNY: Mike, I am hanging over a ledge with this, you know...

MIKE: Yeah, I know. And you could make a big reputation too—

DANNY: Bullshit. This is not for me.

MIKE: Whatever, keep asking..

DANNY: Don't "whatever" me. *(Pause.)* We need to know Mr. Downey, the court needs to know... What was your intent while you were kicking the victim?

MIKE: I was angry, out of control.

DANNY: What was it you were trying to do.

MIKE: In my mind at that time, I think I was trying to get even.

DANNY: For what.

MIKE: I looked at that man. I said to myself: this...this man has a job in this Burger King. I can't even get a job in a Burger King and I see that this man has one. Basically I was blaming him for what was wrong in my life.

DANNY: Good. Do you still feel that way?

MIKE: No. I could probably get a job doing what he was doing.

DANNY: What.. else?

MIKE:	It wasn't his fault. What was wrong in my life wasn't his fault.
DANNY:	Were you trying to hurt him?
MIKE:	Yes.
DANNY:	Would you liked to have killed him?
MIKE:	No. Absolutely not. That wasn't in my mind.
DANNY:	Not even for a minute?
MIKE:	If I had wanted to kill him, he would have died right there.
DANNY:	*(Pause.)* That may be an honest answer but it won't help.
MIKE:	…It's true.
DANNY:	*(Very precisely.)* You need to answer truthfully, you don't need to speculate on what you might have done, had you felt differently. Is there anything else you intend to do while in prison, assuming you go to prison?
MIKE:	I hope to continue to see a psychologist. I hope to continue with studying.
DANNY:	You're doing all right. *(Pause.)* There are a couple of other things to go over Mike.
MIKE:	What else?
DANNY:	I am going to ask you directly, while you're under oath..
MIKE:	Yes..
DANNY:	How can you explain this crime?
MIKE:	I thought you said, don't explain.
DANNY:	Here I'm asking you directly, what do you have to say about the crime..?

MIKE: I.. it.

DANNY: You've prepared something here right? This is what I asked you to do, you agreed.

MIKE: Yeah..

DANNY: Get on with it then.

MIKE: All right. *(He goes through his papers and pulls out some notes.)* Coming as I did, from my particular background.. I had a feeling at that time, that as a White Male I was getting a bad deal..

DANNY: ..How so?

MIKE: There's no hiring incentive for White Males. Not for the fire department, not for the cops, not for any of the traditional jobs for my people..

DANNY: Go easy on talk like 'my people'.

MIKE: Okay, in fact if anything it is just the opposite for the White Male. In those jobs and in many others, in many other areas, we have just the opposite. Even if I go to school like my cousin did, they can't hire a White Male to be a Professor anymore and that is very discouraging.. In all of those jobs that I mentioned, the opposite is true. You have a case where everyone else is considered first...this-by-the-by-is-in-direct-violation-of-the-constitution... Everyone else is encouraged and given a chance over the White Male who is left last...

DANNY: Mike, this is not what I'm after. These are.. excuses. I need an argument..

MIKE: I'm giving you an argument..

DANNY: We've gone over this ground.. I want to hear something new.

MIKE: Okay.. I was coming to place in my thinking where I felt that we had too many immigrants. I was thinking that immigrants were taking over this country, millions per year.

DANNY: WHAT ELSE HAVE YOU GOT?

MIKE   It was my feeling that the White Male had completely lost his pride—

DANNY: Not this shit—

MIKE: I—

DANNY: I don't want this watered-down version of Skin thoughts. I am asking you to tell us, here in the court, why you killed someone? How that happened? What you feel now?

MIKE: I..

DANNY: With everything in that dossier, you can't say anything else? No one else is going to exculpate-

MIKE: Like what Danny? I said I killed him. I said it was wrong, what the hell else am I going to say? You won't hear my defences.

DANNY: Because no one else will hear them. They're not good enough. You have to go to a much greater depth. You've got to get to sinew..

MIKE: I don't want to..

DANNY: YOU HAVE TO. C'mon Mike, for God's sake you must have something else to say..

MIKE: Well.. I could say where I'm sorry for what I did..

DANNY: NOT ENOUGH..

MIKE: Look; I'm on a torture rack here…

DANNY: No, you're.. I have a defence for you. I've built one.. I've worked like a goddamn.. I've worked a lot.

MIKE: So.. what can I do.

DANNY: Tell me why you killed him, what was wrong with you.

MIKE: (*Almost sarcastic.*) ..What was wrong with me?

DANNY: YES. YOU LITTLE SON OF A BITCH. DON'T GET SMART WITH ME. YOU'RE GOING TO GO TO JAIL FOR TWENTY-FIVE YEARS. You might spend twenty-five years in administrative seg.

MIKE: No. No, no, no, no.

DANNY: WHAT THE HELL HAPPENED IN THAT ALLEY?

MIKE: I KILLED HIM, I KILLED HIM BY MISTAKE.

DANNY: AND WHAT THE FUCK, IF ANYTHING HAS IT TAUGHT YOU?

MIKE: ZIP. ZIP. FUCK ALL, ASSHOLE.

           A silence.

DANNY: You just lost it..

MIKE: I didn't lose it. I just got it. FUCK YOU.

           MIKE comes up out of his chair, standing slowly to full grim military 'attention' position.

DANNY: What? What are you doing?

           MIKE begins to speak as a soldier. Through this section his emotions continue to build. Gradually he comes completely unglued, even as he is trying to hold onto and maintain his logic.

MIKE: I am renouncing my co-operation with the forces of The Zionist Occupational Government..

DANNY: Jesus Mike, what are you talking about?

MIKE: My name is Michael Downey, I am a foot soldier in the Great Aryan Resistance, to the Forces of ZOG.

My rank is that of foot soldier. The ZOG has given me a so-called Social Insurance Number, to track my movements and habits. I refuse to utter that filthy number..

DANNY: Mike..

MIKE: I declare my Undying Membership in the The White Aryan Church, of JESUS CHRIST OUR LORD The Redeemer.

DANNY: *(Sits down at the table his face in his hands.)* Oh no, fuck no.. *(He can't even listen or react to this.)*

MIKE: I declare with Furious White Pride, That the Jew; Jews like the man in this room are holding me, a true Patriot, hostage. I am a political prisoner who is being tortured, and forced to read from documents that are not relevant to my actions as a soldier. It is my firm and ardent belief that The Jews, who are now controlling my every action, monitoring my every word, are *(DANNY's overlap begins.)* The Slayers of Christ Our Lord—

DANNY: I have a shield for you—

MIKE: *(Overlapping.)* The Jew Creatures, the Leaders of all the Lesser Mixed Grey Races, have instigated International Communism, while at the same time Control the World Banking System— *(His breathing is irregular.)*

DANNY: *(Quietly.)* I have a breastplate for you, it is the law of Torah. It is your Bible.

            MIKE is starting to lose his mind. While he can say these words, he has to work hard to believe what he says. As he is speaking, he is collapsing emotionally.

MIKE: I declare my act of Violence to be *not* an Act of Hate, but an Act of Holy Righteous Love. *(Pause.)* A Sensible Compassionate Act of Love and Pride, For The Great White Race. *(Pause.)* The Jews, are the

Spawn of Satan, *(Pause.)* descended of Cain and must head.. *(Pause.)* the list of all inferior races to be eliminated, *(Pause.)* in order to make a clean, unfilthy world for the return of *(Long pause. MIKE is now crying openly.)* CHRIST OUR LORD The Redeemer. The only way to stop the Murder is by killing. The killing is perpetrated first and foremost by the Jews, and so, first and foremost, they must be killed. Then will come the inferior.. In this trial I am as an innocent lamb, to the slaughter...

DANNY: *(Roars.)* FOOT SOLDIER DOWNEY, STAND UP STRAIGHT.

MIKE: *(Crying.)* I will not cooperate with the forces of the ZOG.

DANNY: Soldier, I am commanding you to stand up straight.

MIKE: SIR, YES, SIR!

DANNY: What seems to be the problem?

MIKE: Six months in administrative seg.

DANNY: Do you not like administrative seg.

MIKE: No, sir. It's making me lose all of my mind.

DANNY: I want to save you from twenty-five years—

MIKE: Twenty-five years—

DANNY: You have to sit at this table and read this document.

MIKE: Sir, who are you sir?

DANNY: An Officer.

MIKE: An Officer of who?

DANNY: Her Majesty, Queen Elizabeth the Second of Great Britain, an Officer of the Queen's Court.

MIKE:	Sir, yes, sir. Sitting down sir.
DANNY:	I want you to read this.
MIKE:	I've read it, sir.
DANNY:	I want you to read it out loud, please.
MIKE:	I don't know if I can do that, sir.
DANNY:	I happen to know for a fact that you can.
MIKE:	I've read it, sir.
DANNY:	Not for me, you haven't.
MIKE:	Why?
DANNY:	You may be required to do it in court.
MIKE:	If I don't…?
DANNY:	You will be held in contempt.
MIKE:	I'll try, sir.
DANNY:	No. You will do it.

MIKE reads: the speech is agonizingly hard for him to say aloud. Towards the end he struggles to speak and is gradually overcome by the content of what he is reading.

MIKE: Statement: I am at present mostly immobilized in hospital. The brain injury which I have been caused, together with my back, disallows me to walk, or move in a regular fashion. I cannot stand, nor can I properly sit. In general I have the appearance of a man mauled by an animal. Lastly I have difficulty seeing from one eye and only hope for better. I am still in intensive care in case of more complications from the attack. My wife and two children live now in some fear for their lives. They are not, at present, secure. It is my greatest hope to regain wellness, that I may be of some utility again to my family, and all the rest of society. I give thanks to those who have been so much help to me and pray for them that they may be rewarded for their efforts. *(Pause.)* As for the young man who attacked me with no provocation whatever on my part; I feel this young man must be kept from society until a time when he has had a full rehabilitation and is again able to live in a society with many colours. In his Christian Bible; it is Joseph who has a cloak of many colours and this is what we find in all of life. He may one day wish to pick up that cloak for himself. Finally I wish to say to him that, I bear him no grudge in any way. Though I am not a martyr, and take no pleasure in this incapacitation which is not of my doing; if I am destined to die, leaving behind this world, as a Hindu it is my great honour to offer him my forgiveness in a world where forgiveness doesn't exist in many times. I wish him only goodness, comfort, and shade, in this most difficult walk; which he has embarked on, through the many harsh days and nights which can at times be life. I hope as well, that in future he finds a better walk to have. In Heaven and Heaven alone can each be judged according to his merits or demerits..

He begged me...not to, he begged...and I just couldn't... *(Completely loses his breath.)* Holy fuck, holy fuck, holy fuck, holy fuck, holy fuck.

> *MIKE gets up, unstable on his feet, he is reeling. He looks as though he is about do something enormously violent; but instead falls down to his knees, clutching clumsily at a black rubber waste basket. He vomits at length into the bucket. DANNY, watching this display, is agitated to the extreme. He picks up the wooden chair which he had placed for Elijah and by its back and with one gesture, shatters it over the top of the table. MIKE looking up from the last of his vomiting.*

MIKE: *(Meekly.)* ..What the fuck are you doing?

DANNY: I-am-controlling-myself. *(He is holding what is left of the back of the chair, in a directly physically threatening gesture.)* Stand up.

MIKE: What?

DANNY: Michael, stand up. *(Indicating the remaining chair.)* Sit in that chair. *(MIKE does so.)* Now; read the document again.

MIKE: ..What the fuck are you doing to me?

DANNY: Read it. No crying. No whining. No puking. Just read the document.

MIKE: What are you trying to do?

DANNY: I am taking you through the eye of a needle, you are the thread. Once you've gone through that eye, you can decide..

MIKE: Decide what?

DANNY: What part of the fabric you want to be.

MIKE: Where the hell are we?

DANNY: That's what it's all made of—society, reality, time. It's all of it, the threads of a cloth. A divine cloth. You want to be a lone thread? Go ahead. You want to rip that fabric, go at it.

MIKE: I don't know what the hell you're talking about anymore..

DANNY: You want to believe that I'm your "ZOG rep". That's your choice. You want to stick with your fucking hatred you can, God knows we've all got some measure in us.. First you do this. Then you can decide.

MIKE: I have some good in me... Some small good.

DANNY: I don't doubt it...

MIKE: You do, you do doubt.. Where the hell am I? You
              don't even know who I am.

DANNY: I know exactly who you are.. I know your name
              and how to say it. Michael, Michael Downey.

MIKE: Jesus.. What.. What am I supposed to do now?

DANNY: Read the document like a grown-up, full voice,
              everyone will want to hear you. You're in your
              twenties, you're not a boy anymore.

MIKE: All right, all right. "I am at present mostly immobi-
              lized in hospital. The brain injury which I have
              been caused, together with my back, disallows me
              to walk..."

              Lights out on the scene.

Title on screen:

The Fifth Day
One Week After Passover
The Passage of Seven Days

Visual image: Seven tulips.

Scene One

The Passage of Seven Days. Two pools of light rise on a very slow count; isolating the two men, both standing in silence breathing audibly. First breathing with their individual rhythms; DANNY in a breathing pattern of anger. MICHAEL in distress. Over the course of one minute, their breathing comes to be completely in synchronization through their catching each other's rhythms, and balancing their respective breathing on the seventh breath; and finally just before the end of a very long fade out; their breath becomes inaudible.

Scene Two

DANNY and MICHAEL speak the following to-
gether; MICHAEL is heard above DANNY.
Through the speech DANNY's voice fades, until
only his lips are moving with breath and towards
the end, they are completely still.

MICHAEL: My name is Michael Downey. These are my own
             words, which I have put together. I have had help
             only to make the phrasing from Mr. Daniel
             Dunkelman, who is my legal counsel. First off, I am
             asking from the court, for a penitentiary sentence
             of seven years, which is in keeping with quite a bit
             of case law, where people have committed crimes
             like mine, as I did. Next, as a condition of my pa-
             role, should I be offered the chance of parole down
             the road, I would like it made clear that I should
             have it only on the condition that I have some com-
             munity support going out. The Court, I will sug-
             gest, has an obligation to go beyond simply incar-
             cerating me. I present a very particular problem to
             this Court (and to this society). If you ignore this
             problem or try to deal with it, simply by incarcera-
             tion it will not go away. It will simply get worse, is
             all. If you the Court, the people of this society, turn
             a blind eye to this problem, not only will it not go
             away, it will get forever worse. It will break the
             back of your society. Moreover this problem will
             then be yours, and partly your fault too, for having
             ignored it. If there were one of who I was, it would
             be too bad. Ten would be a problem. I am telling
             you from first-hand knowledge that there are tens
             of thousands worldwide. I wish to emphasize that
             I had no intention to kill the man that I killed. There

are others, who even now as you sit here, plan to kill with certainty, and without apology. What you have, on your hands, is a war. How do you ignore such a problem with the lessons of history behind you? Too many young people, young men and women find themselves with no options, with no possible way to move forward in life, they blame and get angry for there not being some good road open to them. You the society must reach to those young people before they get to a point of such desperation and such hatred that they will no longer deal with you or your society. As for me, incarceration will keep me off the street, but that is all. I am safer now in prison for myself and for my society. I ask for something more difficult than simple jailing. I ask for the tools of rehabilitation to be made available to me. I intend to speak against my actions regardless of the outcome of this trial. I have admitted my guilt and do not ask you to excuse it, or forgive it. I ask you simply to see enough of the problem as not only mine but also somehow, slightly yours, that something be done about it. The hand of hatred, the foot, the weapon will not be defeated simply with equal force but only and forever, always with the intelligence which some of you have had the good fortune through yours days to come into the possession of. That is all, thank you for listening to me.

Title on screen:

The Sixth Day
Mid-July

Visual image: A full field of wheat.

Scene One

DANNY is sitting silent in a pool of light, a Cuban cigar in one hand, a lighter in the other. He sits, not saying or doing anything, for a time. He sparks up the lighter, as though to light his cigar. He brings the flame toward his face. He clicks the lighter shut. Lights out.

Scene Two

MIKE: I uh... I can't stop smoking. Every morning I wake up at about five-thirty. I wake up scared, all I can think about is...the stupid things I've done in my lifetime so far. *(Short pause.)* Seven months now, administrative seg. I wake up, I light a cigarette, smoke three, four, five, cigarettes. *(Pause.)* It's guiltiness that does it. I'm not proud of this. No one knows it. No one sees it. It's just me doin' it alone. Same thing after breakfast. It gets better as the day goes by. By lunchtime I'm okay, smoke less. *(Pause.)* I see the psychologist once a week. He's working on my head, to see, to help me see what made me do what I did. Really, I'm working on my head. Also there's some time where I do A.A. in case that's a problem. I've been reading a lot. Material that Danny gave to me. To look at the point of view of other people who were racists; who had a change, who took or found a change of heart. They have a lot to say to me especially, those guys. Because, I was there. I had the respect, or what they think of as respect. I read history too, to balance my view from the education I had as a skin. *(Pause.)* My room is very tight. I'm not complaining about that at all. I'm just saying... A stainless steel sink, a toilet, a bed, different things. I'm living better than I've lived on the outside, the meals. I do seventy-five push-ups, seventy-five sit-ups every day, before supper. The best part, that's seeing the psychologist, it's seeing Danny... From one o'clock to three I'm always in one place. I'm on my bunk in boxers. Got permission especially. The sun hits my window.. ultra-violets break down the ink, a little at a time. *(Pause.)* I'll always be left with white marks. I'll always see that.

Scene Three

Lights up on a federal prison interview room.

MIKE: I haven't been able to reach you for months.

DANNY: I haven't been reachable for months. Deliberately so.

MIKE: What happened to you?

DANNY: Lots.

MIKE: Like…?

DANNY: I needed a break..

MIKE: Why?

DANNY: I was promoted at work. I'm a full partner, I basically get my choice of cases.

MIKE: You needed a break from that?

DANNY: You gonna listen, talk or question?

MIKE: A bit of each.

DANNY: Listen. That's what I need.

MIKE: Oh.

DANNY: The partners said there are better things for me to do now than legal aid.

MIKE: You're talented.

DANNY: The media attention we got, it solidified my career, it's put me in another league.

MIKE: Good.

DANNY: ..Listen.

MIKE: Go ahead.

DANNY: ..My wife left me.

MIKE: She did?

DANNY: Yes.

MIKE: Why?

DANNY: She was tired of me.

MIKE: That's tough.

DANNY: Yeah. Tough.

MIKE: What was her name?

DANNY: Her name was.. her name *is* Anna, she's still alive..

MIKE: I'm sorry.

DANNY: It's not your fault.

MIKE: I didn't.. Did you think it was my fault?

DANNY: I blamed you. The time you took. I blamed every-
           one and anyone but myself. *(Short pause.)* Then I
           blamed myself. It's no use.

MIKE: Do you know what it was?

DANNY: She told me she was tired of being married to a
           bad-tempered, middle-aged man.. who is married
           to his work.

MIKE: That stings.

DANNY: I was in bed for two months.

MIKE: You're better now?

DANNY: I fell to pieces.

MIKE: And now?

DANNY: Now I'm walking around in a stupor.

MIKE: You can't do anything with it.

DANNY: What do you mean?

MIKE: It will take a long time.

DANNY: And then?

MIKE: Eventually, over the course of time, you forgive yourself to some small extent. You start to find pleasure in small things.

DANNY: I still can't work. This is the first thing I've done in three months.

MIKE: And you still have your job?

DANNY: They want my name on the letterhead. Looks good now. I made a name on you.

MIKE: You're lucky you still have the job. That's good.

DANY: I'm not sure I want it. There are a lot of occupational hazards. The lifestyle stinks.

MIKE: You're well paid, you told me so.

DANNY: I don't know what she expected, she knew I was engaged to the practice of law. It's intense.

MIKE: What will you do now?

DANNY: Spend a week at my parents' cottage. Go back to work.

MIKE: I've made some changes.

DANNY: My secretary summarized your letters.

MIKE: You couldn't read my letters..

DANNY: I find myself staring into a dark.. a debilitating endless riddle—beaten by the meaning of everything. I find a taste in my mouth that's what? I don't even want to know. *(Short pause.)* I try to pray and instead I find myself hating you.

MIKE: And your ideas—your eye of the needle…

A silence.

DANNY: Yes. *(Short pause.)* The briefcase…

MIKE: You can't have it back. It's got my homework in it. Grade eleven…

DANNY: It's yours. I want you to have it.

MIKE: Thank you, Daniel.

Title on screen:

The Seventh Day
Harvest, Succoth

Visual image: A 'harvest table' covered with fall harvest vegetables.

Scene One

DANNY: I'm driving on Bloor Street. I'm in my Volvo. I'm trying to drive fast. I'm at Bathurst. I stop at a red light. Some kids try to clean my windshield with their little squeegees, buckets of waste water. Their 'uniforms' are confusing to me. Twenty-one different colours of hair, in different forms. Metal, pierced through lips, leather. An atrocious array of clothing. What does it mean? Who are these strange people? Punks of some sort. A swastika with a red circle and a line through it. No smoking? *(Short pause.)* No Nazis. *(Pause.)* Why is my reaction to their wanting to clean my windshield so visceral and frankly violent? *(Pause.)* I wanted a small piece of.. redemption for Michael so badly, I was willing to beat it out of him with the broken back of Elijah's chair. *(Pause.)* These seven threads comprise a cloth: Spirit, Light, Time, Space, Birth, Death and the Seventh Thread which is the Mystery of the Universe. The un-nameable name which enlivens the dance. This Seventh Thread is also the opposite of Spirit, the opposite of Light, the opposite of Time, the opposite of Space, the opposite of Birth, the opposite of Death. *(Pause.)* It is only the interplay, the movement between all these threads, which creates the Dimensional Known and

Unknown Universe. The Seven threaded Dimensional cloth, which is the very fabric of the Un-nameable. The Fabric extending out from any point, of our Universe. *(Pause.)* The fabric must always be free to move, the threads must interweave and dance through one another; in all their dimensions. That is the only richness in the fabric. *(Pause.)* This movement, this animation in the cloth is: *The Divine Dance of Eternity. (Pause.)* I'm on Bloor Street, in my car. Water streams down my windshield. Sudsy and grey, tired water of a thousand washings. I go to hit the wiper switch arm, to get these fucking kids off my car. What am I thinking? I hate these kids; no, not exactly, I'm afraid of them. I look at them in all their ugliness, in all their confusion, in all their begging state, and I try to reserve judgment on their lives; on my own life; on that of Michael; on those of they I know, and I leave it to another.

Scene Two

MICHAEL: After the trial, I had a certain amount of the media spotlight. I had one day of fame. Reporters and camera people and everyone putting microphones in my face, and putting me onto TV and radio, all over. I used those few minutes to say how there is a big problem which won't go away without tolerance. *(Short pause.)* I know now, it's not tolerance, but love, actual love. It's not good enough to tolerate, you lose it. People suggested to me many times, that I was speaking out against Skinheadism for my own purposes, to show what they call "contrition". *(Pause.)* I'm in jail. *(Pause.)* I knew I'd be in jail. I'm not required to be contrite. I said what I said, because of meaning it. I meant it more than any other thing I had said in my life until that time. *(Pause.)* In jail, I'm working at myself. I'm working to become some kind of new person, who isn't who the old one was. I have good days in jail and bad days in jail. Same as anyone, same as anywhere. *(Pause.)* I'm on the anti-racist coalition web site. I'm listed as a "former Skinhead". I don't like that name, but I'll live with it, if it helps to get the message out. I like to think of myself more as a "former normal person" who took a walk down a very bad, very wrong road. I'm looking for shade, now. The quiet side of the street, a quieter life. Something simpler. Some balance. I don't really have answers much, I have questions. Questions for people who think hate can be put in place for love. It doesn't make it easier for me to speak against Skins. They got Skins in prison, same as everywhere else. Soon they won't even be Skins anymore, they'll get a new uniform; maybe a nice corporate suit and brogues. If I could stop one young person from going down the road I went down... *(Pause.)* For that, I would gladly give my life. *(Pause.)* Prison's a place same as any other, the locks are easier to see. And the closed doors. *(Pause.)* I had to ask myself some hard questions through this. For someone to judge me, that person would have to go through what I went through, and not before. I had to ask myself: if this man Daniel, Danny, if this man is willing to help me, is it really possible that this man is the spawn of Satan? I had to ask myself: who is like Satan? I had to ask myself: who is like the Opposite? *(Pause.)* In prison, I will be no harm to anyone. One day, I will get out, I will be set free. I think and I dream towards that day; and the thing I say to myself when I'm walking back and forth, pacing in my cell is: I hope and I hope and I hope and I hope and I hope and I hope, I hope.

Visual image, seven lit candles.

Title on screen:

Epilogue

MICHAEL: An archangel whose name is a rhetorical question meaning "Who is like God?", Michael is sometimes thought to have fallen, to have been bound to the Devil and later released. Michael is referred to in the book of Daniel: "[Then shall] Michael, stand up."

DANIEL: Whose name means: "God is my judge." He is representative of the idea that we might change the world through righteous prayer. Daniel is thrown into a Den of Lions and is entirely unharmed. Daniel interprets the dreams of his king and saves his king from insanity.

The End.